WATER SONG

WATER SONG

Michael S. Weaver

UNIVERSITY PRESS OF VIRGINIA
Charlottesville

Some of the poems in this collection have
appeared in the following periodicals: *The Baltimore Sun-
papers, Callaloo, The City Paper of Baltimore, Gargoyle, Hang-
ing Loose, Nethula Journal, Piedmont Literary Review,
Signature,* and *The Southern Review.*

Front Cover Art by David C. Driskell

Front Cover Design by Kim Popwell

UNIVERSITY PRESS OF VIRGINIA
Charlottesville

CONTENTS

IN THE SHADOW OF PINES

NIGHT SONGS OF THE CHILDREN

Such were the scenes on Vulcan's shield: Aeneas saw only art, not history, and in joy shouldered the fame and fortune of his sons.

—*The Aeneid,* Book VIII

The sons of God saw that the daughters of men were fair; and they took to wife such of them as they chose. The Nephilim were on the earth in those days, and also afterward, when the sons of God came in to the daughters of men, and they bore children to them. These were the mighty men that were of old, the men of renown.

—*Genesis,* 6:2 & 4

I'm a slow walker, but I'll walk you down.

—*Anonymous*

IN THE SHADOW OF PINES

I'm gonna do right until I feel like doing wrong,
and that won't be long.

— *Otis*

I'm a Christian woman!   I stand for right!

— *Elsie*

BORDERS

I have seen lines on a paper
turn four lane highways to roads
snaking through clusters of pine,
raise foot high grass in medians,
pull the tongues of people to a drawl,
tighten the air and fill it with honey,
put the hands of women on their hips,
stand them in peanut fields with straw hats,
slow the paces of men to a crawl and sit
them on the gas pumps of one room stores,
scratch belligerence in the eyes of whites.
I have gone south in summer nights,
watching the sun rise haughty and oppressive.
I have felt God tinker with man's differences,
moving through our quartered spaces,
making strangers of the same flesh and blood.

A POEM FOR UNCLES

You give the orders, ten two by fours,
a burlap bag split seam to seam
under the maple trees, behind the picnics,
crawling around our projects like paraplegics.
I obey and hammer our tobacco slides
one by one until they stand stout, the bag tight,
the whole array worthy of your mules, ancient,
plodding through muddy furrows headlong,
slapping the leaves on the five foot plants,
bustling with the thick, waxy smell of tobacco.
I worship it like a car while you grow impatient,
slip Prince Albert handrolls between my eyes
as a craftsman. Each cut is precise, each nail
an act of love, my hand steadied to aim
before I wield it violently, smash the thin metal
through the wood. The mules asleep, stupid and
overworked in the barn. If I had not held you
as a god with your flintlock rifles and overalls,
community churches and voodoo, had not seen the light
shimmering past your head in the shadows of watermelon
pig-outs, there would have been pain when you flew away,
a senseless loss like the manmade lake all around us,
water skiers laughing, sliding past the old tobacco
barn, the mules — obedient, indignant, heartbroken.

A TIN ROOF SONG

The music is a tap dancer's sliding soft shoe,
a regimen of holy roller churches where pastors hold
the pulpit swinging the other hand freely, receiving
the Holy Ghost descending. In the house the music
settles frazzled, black farmers — in Africa under
the stupor, the glaze of hunger, in America under
a driving will to be. Harder the rain falls,
darker the night rolls beneath a moon
full of memories, ancestral. Music from rain incites us
to dance, clay-stained, black toes wiggle in sleep to thunder,
a steady slurping of rain falling in sand,
a slow clap of wooden screen doors as dogs retreat.
Lightning cracks on far sides of fields,
splitting edges of forests, lighting tree tops.
An unfamiliar ritual has begun, a past is incarnate,
a West African mask with eyes like black lips
mounted on a sleek, doll body for its divination —
it is the soul of our fathers and mothers.

A KLAN RALLY

In broad daylight,
halfway between Sis Martha
and the grocery store,
in dried earth of a barren
field, they lit a cross,
two wooden beams in rags,
the edges roaring, turning black.
White leprechauns in pointed hats
scurrying at the base, urging
a condolence from the Lord,
sympathy for a world debased.
Pulling the curtain slowly aside,
Sis Martha watched from home,
holding to her bosom, a Bible.
On the inside was a cross of silk,
edged with a blue and white crochet.
Outside — her light brown face, peeking,
looked like a ghost or a devil,
entirely out of place in
the open sun.

EARTH AND VEIN

Like a gypsy snake, free, sullen, cold,
black, curling back, twisting narrow in fits
of whippoorwills dancing on rings, yellow
                golden tubes of Dixie suns.
Down Southampton county and Henrico of Gabriel,
host to tramping gangs of rebellions through
the Carolinas and Kentucky, the whole sweeping
arc of Paradise, rippling the Dixie map like
                supple veins, Southern roads.
Songs under the wheels of wooden wagons,
the rubber, screeching flurry of automobiles,
whispers under bare, marching feet of children,
a rippling crack like quiet thunder splitting seas,
tongue upending beneath Veseys, Turners, Prossers,
                savage murderer, Southern road.

Slain by monsters, the crusaders for freedom,
enlisting the illiterate voters, invading segregation,
shuttling head down to Mississippi lowland to be free,
immersed in waters of baptism by fire of guns,
taken from this world by gun wounds and drowning,
ushered in plush, black velvet of Cadillacs or harsh
                    mule drawn hearses on Southern roads.
Whole families kicking dew against their feet,
following the edges of tar covered paths to fields,
making early morning walks to weed peanuts, prime
tobacco, push their ashy hands in clay to pull unwanted
life from fields in heads wrapped with rags,
leaves of cabbage. Sipping iced water from Mason Jars,
blackening the white life in brick homes and stores,
following the beckoning chant of curves twisting

black and fire hot to their skin around unknown bends
to clearings where hooded vigilantes and prosperous
mulattoes gather in feasts of reunion and plotting,
        on crests of Southern roads.
Shouting and dancing around the wall, crumbling
and rattling the foundation to sway and threaten
its own death, bringing the Lord to war in pine forests,
bursting down through clouds to ride the path of blood
trickling now through the arc of Paradise, the Dixie map,
its supple veins tightening around the heart, drawn tight
        by black hands on Southern roads.

IN THE EVENING SHADE

Isaac, you believe we did the right thing,
packing Henry Lee and Elsie off to Philadelphia,
putting them on Elvira like that. She got her troubles.

The house full, Martha. You know that. Didn't put the garden
in this spring.

I miss my children old man. That's what they is,
chilrens as Uncle Jake used to say. Isaac, can't we...

Naw, woman, naw. I done been over this every evening with you,
and I still say naw. Life is hard and they need to know.

What the Bible say in the Preacher's part? There's time
for everything. It's time for chilrens to be chilrens.

Martha, what we gonna feed em when they start howling.
What we gonna feed em? The dust off this setting sun?
The glow in them old eyes of yours? Your blessed children
love to eat.

Right here, Isaac, it say there is a time for everything,
and over here in Ephesians there is that part about a good
wife. Just you and me and the baby can't manage this place,
make enough to pay for that tractor.

That's a man's worry, Martha.

Yeah and a man ain't much more than a struggling oak without a woman. Just like a rooster that don't know what his gristle is.

Martha, listen. Elvira is your sister.

My half sister.

Yes, but still your sister. Your mother raised you both,
fed you both, taught you right along with the rest of them
children. What you think she gonna do to your brood? Eat em?

It still don't set right with me, Isaac. Them is our children.
I birthed them. If I ain't got a damn crumb, they mine.

Watch your mouth, Martha. The baby'll hear you. This don't
concern her.

Isaac, I want my children. I feel like a star without
its light, just a big empty something hanging in space.
It don't set right with me, Isaac Mason. Don't think it do.

What the Bible say 'bout losing something to gain it?

Ain't no such a thing, Isaac. Jesus said you gain nothing
when you lose your soul trying to get rich, and that's what
I mean. I would rather starve as long as we do it with all
my children here with us. Give John Deere his tractor back.

On Saturday, Martha. We'll go get em on Saturday.

GET HAPPY WOMAN

The queen who stood bugeyed,
arms thrown up and around, flailing,
churning the spirit above her into
an ebony fire rushing the blood in the choir,
as they sang lower and harder.
                There's a bright crown waiting for me
Her hips of stone banging into deacons,
uprooting the heater stove, sliding pews,
her tongue lifting up, out from her lips,
hair flapping with a backward throw of her neck,
her face up with her eyes filling with fear,
a dove's light descending in blue auras,
children sitting silent in fear and wonder,
clutching their grandmother's print dresses,
begging answers in low voices.

"Mama, what is wrong with Fannie"
And the answers came to the children with
stout elbows.
    "Shut up, child. That's the Holy Ghost."
He and her did this dance so pretty,
Him holding her soul with His finger, tipping,
waltzing until she was gone senseless, turning,
popping the blue polka dots on her dress,
standing her up on her heels and back down,
stomping and squatting, twisting and dipping,
an ebony fire rushing the blood in the choir
as they sang lower and harder.
    There's a bright crown waiting for me
This priestess, this medium, this mountain,
this breath from the world of a billion stars,
bringing fire to earth.

THE APPARITION

The time the Lord put His fear
                    in Roy.
He was a chocolate skinned Negro,
not black or the funny light brown,
not Negro at all 'cause his grandfather
was an Indian, big brooding man with
high cheekbones. Roy was the women's
delight until the day he was called
to preach.
He had a partner in Holly Mason, red
Negro from across the line in Carolina,
tall, skinny, mean with green eyes. He
and Roy shared a '62 Chevrolet, white
with beige markings, power steering and
an evil trance on the women to match
Roy and Holly's. In Hezekiah's corn crib,

behind the graveyard, in town
On Saturday nights by the pool room, Roy
and his buddy, Holly, had some mother's
daughter on the run
                    until Roy was called to preach.
They smoked cigarettes and corn silk,
drank white lightning and gin, rode to Richmond
without notice, bought pinstripes
and high collar shirts with cuff links,
loved Sally Phillips, drove the poor gir! crazy,
had others pulling their hair. They were devils
                    until Roy was called to preach.
One Sunday they drank under the dead tree
on the church grounds, hollering and whispering
at the girls, passing the bottle in broad day,
bragging about what they did to Sally P.,
and the sky grew dark all at once on the day
                    the Lord called Roy to preach.

He carries a big hickory stick now,
sets it in the pulpit when he rises,
says it was once a snake like him.
Holy dances, wrestling in the pulpit
with the devil, leaning forward on one
arm, pointing out the backsliders, singing,
preaching, Roy can do it all.
Still he dazzles the women. They get happy,
go into fits — sweating, clapping, gasping
for air, running to the pulpit for Roy
with their arms outstretched, but Holly
is chairman on the deacon board, and
he restrains them with one arm, saying
in his mean, peculiar way,

>   "Politely, sisters, please.
>   Roy's been called to preach."

WATER SONG

In the house that has died,
the dead come down wooden stairs at noon,
puffing the cotton curtain, a cramped bunch
of light pressing down step by step burning,
stopping at the dining room, sitting on
plastic table covers, circling the window,
then they jet through the empty mansion
chasing each other, embracing the empty space
where granddaddy's picture was kept until
the fall from grace, the deaths in the water,
the water of the lake all around the house,
holding the life still there at siege,
jealous mirrors bobbing on small waves that
swallow and fill the lungs with screaming.

No man knows his time, but his time is appointed.

The slipshod mules with box heads and flies,
collar and reins worn to brown frazzle and fiber,
darkened and hardened corn scattered in feed bins,
an empty smokehouse with padlock opened and rusted,
covered outhouse dumps sinking, the old house
flapping its open door back and forth admitting,
garden patch aside going broke under weeds and snakes,
the backporch where we bathed and pinched the girls,
a victorian mansion of wood and tin and screens,
its skin thinning, its bones going hollow and ashen,
its mind blossoming out and over the farm, growing.
Down the path behind the corn crib there is still
the crack of bushes beneath his feet, fallen pine
branches snapping under the crush of his hands,
the restless moan of the mules bemoaning his call,
his call away, the intonation of angels in his ears,
coming down to turn the home into an ugly wailing,
there is still the flailing of arms in lake water,
armies of people in the abandoned home, discarnate.

The dead come back to old folk in the country to talk.

An empty swirl of leaves, empty but for the ghosts,
has fallen in through the window, swirling on the floor,
bronze, yellow gold, black, crisp as paper,
popping up and down on gray, painted floors,
the lives take hold and breathe in the decay,
travelling down the hallway where grandma slept,
gushed by sudden air into the living room where
summer visitors from up north slept and whispered,
back into the kitchen against the hard iron legs
of the stove, they dance and shout echoes,
a shudder in the house and they are gone back,
following evening rays back to the sun, sucking
back to the moon at night, instant glitter
on the roof, then nothing but dull tin and
the evening gossip of angels when the lake
slaps a wet tongue on muddy banks and steep falls.

In the twinkling of an eye, in the twinkling of an eye.

Homemade brooms of straw, bundles wrapped in twine,
skirting the wooden floor, scraping the rough finish,
hands dipping into white, metal wash basins, cupped
in prayer, rubbing against faces grimy with oil,
headless chickens tied to upturned poles, flapping
their wings in anger, feathers filling the yard,
hogs grunting over slop, sleeping in their food,
a pair of hands operating the udder of the cow,
raw milk spraying against the bucket in squirts,
bowl upon bowl of hot vegetables toted to the table,
pot-bellied stove churning an inferno of wood,
in the house that has died and is decaying,
there is laughter, prayer, singing, cursing,
the blare of radios, inordinate snoring from a farmer
who sang his own eulogy as he walked to the lake,
sirens like Egyptian handmaidens over the deepest
move of waves, Canaan in the splashing of catfish,
in the house that has died and is decaying, a shell
of a place where people no longer live in flesh.

Death holds no fear for folk who are Christians.

Grandma sits on the back porch in a metal glider,
riding silently back and forth, cobwebs in the corner,
Her spittoon from a Campbell's soup can
by her foot, through the door comes a sucking
energy like a giant, empty heart with open arms.
She goes again back into the mist of it with
all of them, all the blood of the farm that
has gone to the water and all the plethora
of death, all the endless ways of leaving
in the air over the farm, among the million
blades of grass pushing up, in the clearings
between the pines, a harsh crackle from c.b. radios,
an ambulance starting up from the lake weighed
by a sudden journey to Canaan, through and past
the lake. The life slips free over the fields.

I will be back in the by and by. Dying ain't forever.

In the house that has died,
the dead come down wooden stairs at midnight,
soft feet like cotton shuffling to the front porch,
sitting down to dangle over the edge, examining
the picnic table where children ate watermelon.
Grandaddy sits in his corner, napping, sleeping
in the nest of a big, empty heart, a sucking energy,
a song like Egyptian handmaidens over the lake,
the dark, moving silence around this world.

JESUS HIDES

When the Roman soldiers
were close behind the Lord,
He made himself small like
a shrinking man or a bug.
Then He hid in a pine cone,
silent and small and insignificant,
among the thousands of cones
in the hundreds of trees.
And the soldiers chased shadows,
whispers from cracking twigs,
and the false flashes from their eyes.
When they had gone, he came out,
standing tall on the ground,
the cone still intact, not a wound.
On the inside his hand print
is still pressed in the flesh
of the pine, five tiny fingers
and a palm drawn with his heat.
Now it's in all the pine cones,
among the thousands of cones,
in the hundreds of trees
of the Israel of Virginia.

THE FUNERAL

He comes back from the last one,
in his black pinstripe with the vest,
stands by the window to the street,
curling the leaf of a philodendron in his hand.
    "That was a guy I rode with for twenty years to work."
And I can see the way he stood at the altar,
peeping down into the coffin, feeling top heavy,
afraid to be too affectionate for a shell of flesh,
a thing we are given to use like Cadillacs or sackcloth,
afraid to see if this face too feels like leather.
He takes the program from the services and adds it to
the collection under his old handkerchiefs and phone bills,
sits by the window against the cemetary. No relief from life.
This funeral was like all the others —
a sermon where they mention how Lazarus got
to the council of patriarchs in heaven and went to sit,

all the folk in the congregation wondering what a patriarch is,
how Lazarus got there and got comfortable when Jesus
   shouted,
        "Lazarus."
And Lazarus got downright angry with the Lord's indecision.
       "'Hush up," he said, "Damn it! I'm dead!"
And death works that way. You get all settled in a new body
thin as air and full of flight. That last thing you want is
          a pardon.
But funerals are heavy with all the things the living must bear,
all the weight that sits in the pews and watches your victory,
half in fear, half in jealousy, all in apprehension.
And some come like my father, all reverent and proud,
humbled by the cacophonous wail of old women in the choir,
moved by the off key refrains to single teardrops.
   I'll fly away.

And that starts him to remembering the half-hour prayers
on ten year old knees beside his oldest brother, who is now
    in flight,
against the breasts of his mother who went smiling,
walked right into heaven knowing everything, like Enoch
    almost.
And it starts him to feeling again like the last warm touch
he had from his wife in a hospital morgue. The old midwives
who brought him to this shell of clay walked with his wife to
    Jordan
where she played like a small girl.
He remembers many songs, many things that have abandoned
    life.
    I know he didn't bring me this far to leave me.
And he sits by the window and wonders when it will come,

when will the night smash against the window like a wave of
    an ocean,
fall down in streaks that arise and sing.
    O, there's a voice in the shadow in the field.
    Come on in son. I believe it's gonna rain.
And it doesn't help to talk about heart attacks,
or the way people freeze like unborn children in a world
    of plenty,
or whether there is a heaven, or how close,
and I dare not mention how I feel like a god.
He hangs his suit back in the closet slowly, precisely,
wondering why funerals are at night. Philadelphia style,
   * they say.
He wonders why he has to come back and sit in the chair
    at night
to wash away the howling that comes out of the front pews,
mixing with bittersweet accounts of Lazarus,

turning his hands one over and against the other, wondering
how the slow pulse and sweat can go thick and rough like old
    hide,
thinking how nice it is to sleep. And the bed sits beside him,
empty and white, as all of a sudden he is full of fear.
He looks into the night wondering if it might be a horseman,
or a gathering shout that swells in the distance like an
    oncoming
light of silver candescence, or like someone else
who was taken away calmly by his Aunt Martha, who was just
    there
when they opened their eyes. They have told him this
    in a dream.
He comes back from each funeral this way,
and each time I am lost for consolation, not able to say,
"I know what it is to die."

NIGHT SONGS
OF THE CHILDREN

Do you know what they mean when they say
in the twinkling of an eye?

—Jesse

A YOUNG ARISTOCRACY

On their weekends off from the mills,
my father and uncles drove their new cars
to Turner's Station, the mill smokestacks
in the distance, their lungs still feeling
the scratch of the soot they took for air —
in three and two piece suits with big shoes,
their Virginia and Carolina ways in a big city.
My mother and her sisters sat on the porches,
in white dresses with ankle socks and patent
leather like dark images of the Andrews Sisters.
Every day on time and some sixteen hour shifts
paid for the cars, the suits, the promises,
the grand feeling of buying a new rowhome.
It was the best the world would give then
to its best workers, blacks, browns, high-yellows
from the South. It took us children thirty years
to believe it. Now we are grateful.

CURRENTS

The Polish
were always
the bottom rung,
trampled on, mocked.
When the Irish had
clerk jobs on the docks,
the Polish were the coolies,
putting cargo away by hand,
under the snobs of Ireland,
the last totem on the pole.

I remember when we learned the Madison,
all of us in the front living room in a line,
my youngest sister forgetting to save her turn.
We did two up and two back while she spinned,
a big boss turn that threw her in mama's plants.
We had a Webcor high-fidelity in a wooden cabinet.
When the twist came in, it was easier to dance,
each of us claiming our own turf in the rug.

Where they make
porcelain toilets and tubs,
it gets so hot you cry,
thinking of home,
the tears blowing away
the gas and stench.
Many youngsters hollered,
quit and never came back.
A big Polish man gave
my uncle an onion to survive.
"Put this around your tongue, boy.
It'll help you keep your job."

Some things never change. Powers and principalities rise,
mass movements topple laws, but money still talks and buys.
With overtime come cars, tailored suits, Florsheims.
Black men leave their smokestacks and conveyor gears
on Saturday. They get a close barber shop shave,
a spit shine on all leather shoes, an Italian knit shirt.
On the street they pad a single fifty with a wad of ones.
The world never changes because they too often forget it.
On Monday they're back with bad heads and poverty.
Powers and principalities rise, mass movements topple laws.

Gas from coke ovens
makes you sleep,
not sickly or pale,
just long, deep sleep.
On the graveyard shift
it's a steel dagger in silk.
At home you darken a room,
turn the air conditioner on,
hide your head in blankets.
When you awake,
the light is gone,
darkness takes you again.
The gas is gone out
in the day, having killed.

For some old time women, nothing was enough,
not the home with shag carpet, paneled bedrooms,
custom built kitchens, leather coats for the kids.
They drove their men to work to escape them.
Sixteen hour shifts, on a loading dock, conjure women,
wet the tongue for bourbon, scotch and gin,
and it was always some light-skinned heifer in town.
On some weekends he disappeared for three straight days,
in another bar with another angry woman pouting,
her patent leather high heels curled on her toes,
a tiny waist and firm breasts in a 5th Avenue dress.
In the mirror he shakes his head and cries in his hands.

Nobody ever told us
white folk had a head start,
knew the deal before us.
They built homes
when we sported the crowd.
At a company benefit
they all wore white socks.
It was insurance money
old folk left them, we heard.
All we know is
their stumbling blocks
are few on a well-lit path.
Black folk lie on beds of nails.
Waking, they walk on cobblestones,
never a break from the aching.

After forty-five years, you fight for your pension.
At the union hall young men barter for a strike,
rattling your old nerves to shaking and breaking.
In a closed ballot you vote to give them what you had,
a fair start — their health and Providence against the company.
Then you wait, forgetting gratitude and fear, you wait
for the monthly checks, the long evenings, the dusk.
You force a stern, still eye on those behind you.

Was a time
the Germans
were all over Baltimore.
Once they covered
where blacks have ghettoes.
In Druid Hill Park
they had their picnics,
their rowboats in the reservoir.
Black people worked for them.
The Germans
were all over Baltimore.
They were above
the Irish, the Polish
who sweated on the docks.

When your mother went to Pikesville as maid and nanny,
sweaters and pants and shirts came down free, donated
from the solid cherry and maple dressers of young master.
On the weekend leftover food came also to Bronzeville,
wasted shrimp, piles of sliced prime beef, strange vegetables.
Nobody explained this shame to us children, these handouts.
It was a blessing we thanked the Lord for on our knees.
Twenty years hence the clothes are tight, the food tastes
        strange.
We remain close to Earth, earning grace with sacrifice.

PARADISE REVISITED

In the South now,
they work in factories,
leaving the wooden houses
and fields of corn
to put eight hours in pulp mills.
Farms are too small
to bring in the big money.
All day on a tractor
on seventy-five acres
is nothing except close to God,
the poverty of clothes worn smooth and thin.
Shelling peas and canning
are done in leisure time now,
some fields go unweeded,
hogs are down to one sow,
all but three sucklings are sold.
Men and women come home
to stand motionless
in the silence for a while,
to forget the noise, the clutter.
In the evening old farmers
relax the way they always have —
lying down, on their porches
barefooted; stray cats watching,
dry flies singing in the trees,
chickens clucking and strutting
while the air turns and tumbles;
sucking pine needles
along a velvet tongue.

BABY BOY

Baby Boy is a veteran,
his bad leg, his paunch are scars.
He remembers when South Baltimore
was hell and risk for blacks at night;
he has rolled the world to snake eyes
on the black side of Pigtown bars.
Sweat creeps now from fibers of gray hair.
He curls his cigarettes from hidden smiles,
now that the streets are safe to walk
with small twenty-twos and straight razors,
now that black folk are not playthings,
now that curses come from under breath,
as fire snorting from deep down like a snake.
Baby Boy outstrips the youngsters, loading
trucks, soaked in his own water, limping.
Now that we don't have to hold back,
Baby Boy goes through Pigtown in a new car,
his cap turned sideways and down, for business.
Baby Boy is a warrior.

A PHOTOGRAPH OF NEGRO MANIA

Sitting on cracked and peeling marble steps,
riding in worn out limousines hanging over the chassis,
struggling up city street hills waddling with
sweating backs, exposed to overeating and ads and ads and ads,
fist sized hearts imprisoned, sentenced to beating
through uncharted miles of untoned and suicidal flesh
                    whispering, "Lord."
Whispering "Lord" over and over, turning fish in pans,
beating the rising dough, filling pie shells, feeding
starving masses flashing through alleys like ricochets
of lasers, standing on swollen ankles, radios crackling
                    with morning spirituals.

Stages with mohair suits and precison dancing,
artistic genius with classic starvation setting jazz
to geometric progression, crazy men in African zoot suits
with saxaphones, the lead given to bass players when the leader
falls in a pool of sweat, vibraphones beat with blinding
flurries of minute and hairy tongs, the songs, the greatest
                    burp of childlike people.
On trains with cardboard suitcases filled
with fried chicken, potato salads making greasy eyes
on the sides, peeping Southern eyes on the passengers, the North
whipping past the windows in a blur of trees, coming in 1902,
1943, 1960 and before there was ever a clock or civil rights
worker to count them, coming in pre-Columbian trinkets
to lie in Cuba in shallow graves and the bottomless hells
                    of the Smithsonian and cultural indignance.

Thirty million of them whooping and dancing on the head of a pin,
under the eye of Jesus, their preachers the epitome of Saturday
night conmanship, their mahogany elegance a tune in four four,
the haphazard za-zen of classical Bach and heathen jungle drums
suddenly becoming percussion.
Unashamed, unashamed, unfree and brought up right,
respecting the smooth glow of moonshine and stars,
the striking stink of rubbing alcohol cooling their grandmother's
heels in her winters, the Beatitudes and poison ivy in vacations
in the hell of the South.
Sitting quietly, still as pre-storm summer air,
taking frozen, homemade kool-aid popsicles, making them last,
turning fried eggs without breaking in grease of week old bacon,
bending our skin shiny heads saying evening politely to the age
and darkening white shadows.

Up the one lane highways through the Carolinas and Virginia,
bouncing on shifting droplids of Chevrolet pickups,
turning paper fans for four hours on Sundays, eyes peeled back
at the boredom, occasional madwomen doing foot stomps
in the aisle, the Holy Ghost descending in a curtain of raining
tears, settling on the mouths chewing gum and love notes,
                    up through gates to heaven.
In another spring, renewed, full of insight, humbled,
blackness is something revered, falling on unwilling hearts
like the cloak of night — this misery, these smiles unsummoned
in the alleys, rusted Cadillacs, fish frys, church dinners,
dark bars shooting dice and drinking wine, dying, falling out,
                    making a grand appeal to Jesus.

SOUTH AFRICAN COMMUNION

It is not difficult to feel compassion
for the workers in South Africa that stand
in half mile lines waiting to board buses,
down the dirt roads of shanty towns to mines
and auto factories, the hats with headlights
passing ore up to the bosses, tight-lipped
and fervently religious with their usurpation
of God. At night in South Baltimore we take
excursions from company property to the bars
downstreet, the convenience stores in the heart
of white condolences. The faces we meet, the blank
smiles, the beckoning fists, the yells are
grandchildren of laws that did not allow blacks

to set dusty foot on white pavement past nightfall,
did not allow excursions, the wooly growths to be
called afros, or brown fingers grasping books —
nothing pretentious and black but the night itself.
It is not difficult to understand greed here
where freedom has been harvested, cut and laid aside
to die, when a whole other similar paradise was carved
from theft. The whole arrangement comes clear.
It's the times I look down and see the dark brown,
veiny hands beneath white frowns, or the scowering
shadows of neon lights from seven-elevens and police
sirens, when a waitress would rather not touch my hands

with the change, when a cop calls me *boy* when I'm thirty,
when people force laughter over clenched knives. It's just
a joke and not very difficult to feel compassion
for the workers in South Africa standing mute in predawn,
hustling to houses of relatives and friends at night
with passes underlined with photos, tossing stones at
personnel carriers. It's easy travelling the streets of
Baltimore, searching the shadows for psychotic cops,
clutching the passport licenses to drive and be seen,
against the impregnable shadows of the moon over the
hatred.

THE AFTERMATH

Old men who have given their lives to labor,
thirty years of catering to whims of machinery,
bologna and pot luck soup with hot coffee
against the hollow clang and solid thud of metal.
Now they pass their waiting time in huddles,
crowded around concrete benches in shopping centers,
freight trains wrapping around them like skeletons,
each metal car a bone forming the spine of the city.
Old men rub their hands across arthritic knees.
One does a slow polka, bragging about his still potent sex.

"Aw, Leon. Quit your goddam lying and boasting.
You ain't had a notion in ten good years, like the rest of us."

Another city away, ten blocks across the cemetery,
the solo dance is a stiffened bosa nova in an alley,
a hobbling by old men who have given their lives to labor,
scuttling to *for colored only* bathrooms and lockers,
bologna and pot luck soup with hot coffee,
under the fading whisper of Cab Calloway originals,
played in fearful ears under machinery's din.
Now they pass their waiting time in huddles,
conspiring to cheat death with enthusiasm and courage,
around an abandoned lot cluttered with old cars,
changing this part and that one for this new one,
whistling and gesturing to young women and girls,
dropping wads of money and credit cards to entice.

"Lil Bit. You would have a stroke behind that young stuff.
Your best bet is to lay your ass in the shade and sleep."

In the mills and shops, on the working floors,
down under the holds of freighters in docks and berths,
handling razor sharp edges of tin plate with cotton gloves,
driving forklifts in open warehouses in bitter winter,
mixing the blackened air of steel to paste with Vodka,
loading trucks with forty thousand pound cargo by hand,
sitting under the constant turning, spinning, whirring,
fighting the boredom with naked women, practical jokes and
    Zane Grey,
hands turned from boyish clay to hard stone and ice,
forearms and wrists tightened with extra layers of flesh,
millions of hearts like subtle miracles wielding tears.
Over the years, a world within changed by the world without.
For colored only and *get back nigger* torn away and burned,
savored only by a nostalgia for the illusions of power,
replaced by a democracy of simply men and women,
another step closer to a dream and a nightmare.

"When they hired the niggers, the country fell apart."

When the machine leaves them suddenly, it's like death.
For months, hands, eyes, feet, minds move as always,
turning levers, hauling cartons, pushing brooms that are gone —
the same waking hour in the morning, shaving, hot coffee,
a ritual of early morning small talk with wives and kids;
but now days are empty things to be filled and passed.
In the shopping centers, around junk car lots,
hearts strung with Guy Lombardo and Cab Calloway.
In neighborhood halls filling up on pasta and dumplings,
at a cabaret with barbecue pork and fried chicken,
knotted hands like claws tapping idly on white table cloths,
passing through the waiting time, conspiring to cheat death,
the grave another machine to be tended to, to run.
No one of them will do it alone. The world is full of people.

"The Good Lord got something for this old world. I know it."

Retired black men buy Cadillacs and gigantic Buicks,
take them to bridges and large trees to wax them,
ride through the neighborhood at a snail's pace to signify,
blowing the horn at gray heads on porches and front steps.
They take trips to New York or home to Virginia,
cross the city once or twice to visit their white friends.
There together they laugh and drink Spanish wine.
It has been this long before they have known each other,
known the both are men, this close to the end,
in this slow walking through the waiting time.

TO THE VIETNAM VET

It must have been like a funhouse,
walking the high cliffs under rock apes,
dodging the large stones they tossed down,
lifting the black death to shoo them,
when the women were as cheap as cigarettes,
dutiful, lasting as long as the dollars,
In the jungle night must have felt like
the plumage of a giant peacock around you,
a billion eyes still as pursed lips on
your arms. I remember this when I approach
your house on foot, peeking under cedar
bushes for feet other than the slanting trunk,
taking cover under the first lamp light.
When you peek from your window smeared with
paint, I know it is you and not the black
patriot sleeping in shit with dead men,
remembering Martha & The Vandellas,
afraid to call out to soldiers who
declared it was not your war. Strange
thing when they fire vets from jobs because
they remember, because they stand still
for a moment like sailors tied to a mast,
weathering the storm of phantoms. Stranger
still that I must write a hundred songs
for your unpainted army because I want
you all to believe I understand.

A LIFE IN A STEEL MILL

My father is proud of his life making pipes,
his small rowhome, his five children, his peace,
two week vacations he took in summertime,
hauling us in his '54 Ford to Lawrenceville,
his wife throwing her arm around him.
He likes to think he was able to pay for good times,
crab feasts in public parks, Saturday drinks
with my uncles while his wife cooked hot soup.
He is as steady as a mountain at rest,
in movement he has the force of an inland river.
He believes in the Resurrection and good bourbon.
He is grateful for the life work has afforded.
My father is a burning sun, an oracle of flesh,
the damp crush of morning dew on naked feet,
a crack and screech of wooden wagons in tobacco,
a host of empty echoes like thunder in caverns
of steel mills, the clatter of his buddies
at a roadside bar coming in town from work.
My father is a son of the ten thousand things.
My father is an oak tree, tears I have never seen
come through buds in springtime to become leaves.
My mother in her death is the wind and rain.

A NEW NEPHILIM

After the Lord
laid the world out,
kissed it full with water,
angels made the first life,
coming on the young women
at night singing, rushing
breezes stirring across naked
skin. Giant men were born who
knew all that God knew, becoming
gods themselves, the populated
myths of Greece and Rome. It was
too much. God killed them all
in surging oceans. Their memories —
Ovid's dreams. Now in a
single hundred years, the rape
of night breezes has seeded
the planet with industry,
the thunder the giants made
when they leaped for stars.
God's anger is around us,
seething, swollen with hot breath —
yellow eyes on our disobedience
like bloody fires in the night,
or the eyes of the cats.

Photo by David Hoffman

MICHAEL S. WEAVER

Michael S. Weaver was born in Baltimore, Maryland, in 1951. He has studied at the University of Maryland, Morgan State University, and the State University of New York, where he is completing his bachelor's degree. During the past five years, he has been a free lance journalist, working principally for the *Baltimore Sun*. In addition to writing poetry and non-fiction prose, Weaver is editor and publisher of *Blind Alleys*, a journal of literature, and publisher of 7th Son Press. He is a member of the staff of the Maryland Poets in the School Program and a National Endowment for the Arts Fellow (1985-86).